HERITAGE

The
ROMANS
in Britain

Robert Hull

Heritage

The Anglo-Saxons
The Celts in Britain
The Romans in Britain
The Tudors
The Victorians
The Vikings in Britain

Cover pictures: Hadrian's Wall (main picture). A glass jug and bowl from Radnage, Buckinghamshire (left); a London pavement mosaic (top right) and a statue of Mithras from Hadrian's Wall (bottom right). Title page: The pool at Bath. This page: A St Albans street mosaic.

Editor: Jason Hook
Designer: Jean Wheeler

First published in 1997 by Wayland Publishers Limited,
61 Western Road, Hove, East Sussex, BN3 1JD, England

This edition published in 1999 by Wayland (Publishers) Limited

© Copyright 1997 Wayland Publishers Limited

British Library Cataloguing in Publication Data
Hull, Robert
    The Romans in Britain. - (Heritage)
    1. Romans - Great Britain - History - Juvenile literature
    2. Great Britain - History - Roman period, 55 BC - 449 AD - Juvenile literature
    3. Great Britain - Civilization - Roman influences - Juvenile literature
I. Title
936'.1'04

ISBN 0 7502 2552 1

Typeset by Jean Wheeler

Printed and bound by G. Canale & C.S.p.A., Turin, Italy

Contents

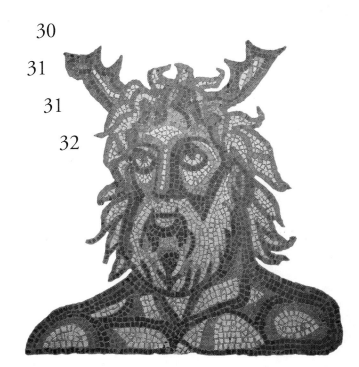

chapter one

WHO WERE
THE ROMANS?

Romans in Cumberland wore underpants. Soldiers camping at Chester ate perch. A million iron nails were stored in a Scottish fort. How do we know? Because a letter – written on thin wood – has been found mentioning a parcel from home with two pairs of underpants. Because a Roman rubbish dump dug up near Chester contained fish-bones, including perch. Because the million nails were found in a pit, hidden there by the Romans to prevent the British making them into weapons.

The Romans left behind them monuments, mosaics, milestones, gravestones, toilets, lamps, pins, bones and jewels. They left lighthouses and forts. We can still see the lines of their long, straight roads; and the rectangular white outlines, like faded tennis courts, of their vanished towns.

▲ *A bronze and silver helmet and mask, found at Ribchester, in Lancashire, where there was a Roman fort. It was not worn for fighting, but for ceremonies.*

The Roman people were originally farmers settled among seven hills in a region called Latium, with a central town called Rome. Gradually this one 'tribe' became powerful, invading the land of neighbouring peoples. By about 270 BC, Rome had conquered most of what is now Italy.

The Roman Empire grew from there. For 200 years its armies marched and conquered. A famous Roman writer called Cicero said: 'Glory in war exceeds all other forms of success.'

Many 'Roman' soldiers were not from Rome at all. They came from Africa, western Asia, and most parts of Europe. A famous governor of Roman Britain, Agricola, was a Celt from Frejus, in southern France. There were boatmen from the Tigris River, and archers from Syria. But so far, no Roman soldiers came from Britain.

▲ *In the 1940s, a farmer's plough unearthed this Roman silver dish at Mildenhall in Suffolk.*

◄ *This Roman road stretches through Wheeldale Moor, Yorkshire. Across Britain, the Romans built 1000 km of long, straight roads paved with local stone. It was said that, 'All roads lead to Rome'.*

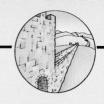

chapter two

WHEN DID THE ROMANS COME TO BRITAIN?

▲ *A Roman coin from the time of Julius Caesar, the first Roman invader of Britain.*

In 55 BC, Julius Caesar tried to invade Britain. The Roman government had sent him to conquer Gaul, the part of Europe centred on what is now France.

Caesar conquered Gaul. But if he had reported his work finished, he would probably have been recalled to Rome, losing command of his army. He also says in his book *The Gallic War* that British Celts had fought against him in Europe. Britain's unfriendly peoples might be a threat to the new Roman province of Gaul.

Caesar also knew that Britain was wealthy. Roman merchant ships had carried wine, glass and other luxuries to the friendly Celtic nobles of Britain for years, bringing back slaves, silver, tin, corn and cloth.

▶ *The Romans imported expensive luxuries into Britain. This glass bowl and jug were found in a grave at Radnage, Buckinghamshire.*

Caesar's first invasion attempt was almost a disaster. His ships were unsuitable for landing. His soldiers struggled ashore through heavy waves and there was brief, confused fighting. In a few weeks, Caesar was back in Gaul.

A year later Caesar tried again, with 800 ships and an army of nearly 40,000 men. This time he landed successfully, and marched inland. But after defeating a large British camp Caesar again returned to Gaul, with hostages and promises of 'tribute' – payments of gold.

The real invasion took place ninety years later. In AD 43, Claudius became emperor. Romans thought he was slow-witted because he stammered, and a cripple because he limped. In fact Claudius was very clever, but he had to prove himself. Conquering Britain would make him popular, as well as adding silver, slaves and even pearls to the great wealth of the Empire.

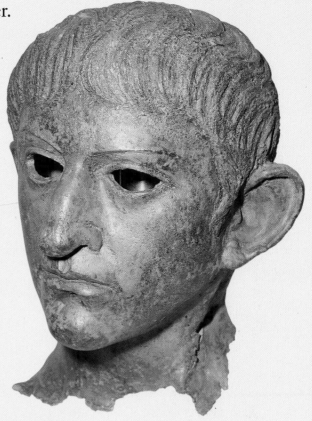

▲ *This bust of the emperor Claudius was found in the River Alde in Suffolk.*

At this time, there was trouble in southern Britain between supporters and opponents of Rome. A British king, Verica, appealed to Claudius for help. This was the emperor's excuse to invade.

Caesar wrote of the Britons: 'Most of the tribes of the interior do not grow corn, but live on milk and meat and wear skins. All the Britons dye their bodies with woad, which makes them a blue colour, and this gives them a terrifying appearance in battle.'

◀ *Buried Roman treasures like this gold ring reveal the wealth of Roman Britain.*

7

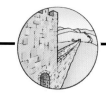

▲ *This piece of Roman scale armour was found in the north of England.*

chapter three

HOW DID THE ROMANS
CONQUER BRITAIN?

Claudius sent his general, Plautius, to 'help' Verica. Well-drilled Roman armies came ashore in Kent and Sussex. The various British tribes were not organized to fight as one army. The Roman writer Tacitus said: 'It is very rare that two or more British tribes will come together to repel a common danger. They fight separately and separately are defeated.'

Plautius' troops marched successfully inland nearly to Colchester. Claudius came over to Britain to lead the final attack, bringing with him, of all things, some elephants!

Claudius was given the title 'Britannicus' and awarded a 'triumph', a magnificent procession through Rome. A triumphal arch was built, and prisoners from Britain were hauled through the streets.

► *The skeletons of mutilated bodies have been found here at Maiden Castle, Dorset, where one of Plautius' armies defeated a group of Britons.*

In south-east Britain, the Roman occupation had begun. But to rule properly, the Romans had to conquer the rest of the island. Their legions seemed unbeatable. The soldiers were highly trained and extremely fit. They practised walking 32 km in 5 hours carrying 22 kg of kit, and fought in organized teams. One famous Roman tactic was the *testudo* or tortoise, in which twenty-seven men advanced under a roof of shields, like an armour-plated scrum.

Even against such troops there was resistance. A number of British tribes combined under a great leader, Caratacus, and fought the Romans beside the River Severn. The British were beaten, and Caratacus fled north to a tribe of Britons called the Brigantians. Their queen, Cartimandua, who was friendly to the Romans, betrayed Caratacus to them. Caratacus was taken to Rome, but so impressed Claudius that instead of being executed, he was pardoned.

Tacitus described the Britons at Anglesey in AD 60: 'Close by stood Druids, raising their hands to heaven and screaming dreadful cries ... it was their religion to drench their altars in the blood of prisoners and consult their gods by means of human entrails.'

▼ *A map of the main stages in the Roman conquest of Britain.*

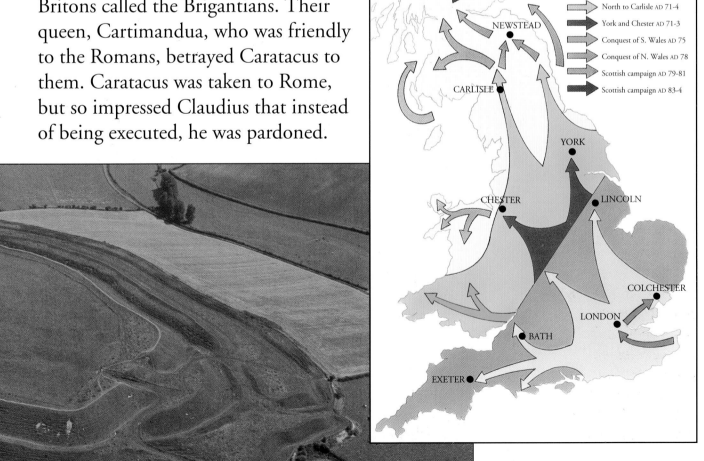

Boudicca

The most famous British resistance came from a tribe in East Anglia called the Iceni. Their king died, leaving the emperor a share of his land; but the Romans behaved as if they now owned the whole territory. Nobles were evicted from their homes and treated as slaves. The king's widow, Boudicca, was flogged, and her two daughters were raped.

Tacitus describes how, led by the enraged Boudicca, the Iceni attacked Colchester, killing everybody in sight. They surged on to St Albans and London, slaughtering and burning. Archaeologists have found burnt material dating from this time at both these places.

Boudicca's force of perhaps more than 200,000 finally came up against a 10,000-strong Roman army. They fought in open country, the Britons dashing about in their chariots, watched from wagons by women and children. The Romans killed 80,000 British rebels, and the defeated Boudicca poisoned herself.

▼ *You have to climb steeply to get to this Roman fort at Hardknott, in the Lake District. It is 300 metres above sea-level, and must have been a fiercely cold place in winter.*

◀ *A silver coin of the Iceni tribe.*

In a letter, one Roman soldier in Britain mentions a 'parcel from home' he received containing socks, two pairs of sandals and two pairs of underpants.

Within a few years, most of England had settled under Roman rule. The Roman fort at St Albans was pulled down in AD 44, as peace brought a Roman-style life to Britain.

The north was still unsettled, and most of Scotland remained outside the Roman Empire. The Brigantian tribe were often troublesome, so the Romans drove them from their hill-forts. The Romans then had to build their own fortifications, to guard against Brigantian raids.

By the early part of the second century, the worst trouble in Britain seemed to be over. Between the second and the fourth centuries, Roman Britain was a largely peaceful province of the Roman Empire.

▼ *Leather sandals, like this one found at York, were first introduced to Britain by the Roman troops who wore them.*

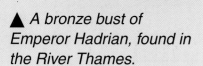

chapter four

HOW DID THE ROMANS TRANSFORM BRITAIN?

When you see Hadrian's Wall you sense the cruel strength of Roman power. The Romans ruled Britain with their superbly organized army, 40,000 to 60,000 strong. Within hours an army of 5,000 men could build a night camp, complete with rampart, ditch, fence and gates. Discipline was fierce. Punishment for cowardice was *decimation*: one in every ten men executed. We still use the word today to mean the destruction of large numbers of people.

The most important frontier was in the north. When Hadrian became emperor in AD 117, the Brigantians were giving the Romans more trouble. To protect Roman Britain from these barbarians, Hadrian ordered the building of a great, defensive wall about AD 122.

▲ A bronze bust of Emperor Hadrian, found in the River Thames.

▼ Hadrian's Wall linked 14 forts and was fortified every mile with garrisons of 100 men. It faced a wild land, and was defended by brute military strength.

Hadrian's Wall took eight years to build. It was 115 km long, 2 to 3 m thick, and up to 7 m high. There was a ditch on the north side 9 m wide and 3 m deep, and another on the south. All along the wall were signal turrets and small forts called milecastles.

The main forts had stables, barracks, parade-grounds, granaries, and baths. Remains of them all can still be seen.

One reason why the Romans were able to control Britain was the roads they built to carry marching soldiers, coaches, heavy ox-drawn supply carts, and horses galloping with Imperial mail. Roman military engineers built hundreds of bridges and fords. They built canals, especially in East Anglia, and deepened rivers.

The army's control allowed the Romans to rule Britain as a province of its empire. The Romans were brilliant at governing, making laws, organizing the local people to do their work and collecting taxes.

One Roman wrote: 'When the barbarians had been dispersed and the province of Britain had been recovered, Hadrian added a frontier-line between either shore of the ocean for eighty miles, to divide the Romans from the barbarians.'

▼ *A map of the main roads and towns of Roman Britain.*

HADRIAN'S WALL

ALDBOROUGH · YORK

CHESTER · LINCOLN

WROXETER · LEICESTER

GLOUCESTER · COLCHESTER
CIRENCESTER · ST. ALBANS

BATH · LONDON
SILCHESTER

—— MAJOR ROADS

▲ *The theatre at Verulamium on the outskirts of St Albans. The crowd sat on wooden seats on the earth banks.*

The British adopted all kinds of Roman habits and fashions. Women in Roman Britain wore make-up: chalk to powder the face, red-ochre for lipstick and ash for mascara.

Roman towns

The work undertaken by the Romans was paid for by the British. Through taxes, local towns paid for the building of roads, rest-houses with baths, horse-changing stations and the horses themselves.

The Romans organized British settlements into different kinds of town. A *vicus* was a trading settlement that developed round Roman military camps. The most important town was the *municipium*, like London which soon became a great commercial city.

The Romans built the first 'modern' towns, with facilities that we take for granted today. They provided water supplies and splendid public buildings. Britain started to *look* Roman. Most towns had a *forum* – a closed-in square with a market, shops and a *basilica*, which was a kind of town hall. Many had baths and an *amphitheatre* – an oval-shaped space, usually at the edge of town, for games and shows.

The heart of Roman power was the basilica, which was adorned with sculptures to show its importance. The basilica included the law courts. Here, a magistrate imposed fines as punishment, or confiscated property. Roman towns did not have jails. In serious cases not only suspected offenders could be tortured – but witnesses too!

Many towns in England had sewage systems. York and Lincoln had a complicated network of main drains serviced by manholes. But drains were a luxury. Other important towns, like Silchester, managed without.

Gradually, from being forced to become Roman, Britain started to become Roman by choice. As soon as Britons started to think of themselves as Roman, Roman control was strengthened. The rule of the Romans brought with it increasing benefits.

In AD 213 all Britons except slaves were made citizens of the Roman Empire. Every free Briton was now a Roman.

Tacitus writes: 'Roman dress came into fashion and togas were worn everywhere. The British people were gradually won over by the temptations of shopping precincts, hot baths and official banquets.' He adds: 'The Britons called these new fashions civilization; but they were only the signs of their slavery.'

◄ *The foundations of the 'hypocaust' at Fishbourne Palace, Sussex. The hypocaust was a system of underfloor heating creating hot water and steam for the bath-house.*

chapter five

WHAT DO WE KNOW OF LIFE IN ROMAN BRITAIN?

▲ *This vase found at Colchester shows two gladiators fighting. The one on the right raises one finger as a sign that he gives in.*

The Roman forum was a bustling and noisy shopping precinct. Shops were often workshops too, selling at the front what they made at the back: bread, shoes, bags, bronze toilet articles, locks, combs, pins, whistles, hinges and dice. There were many British goods: pottery from Poole, glass from Norfolk, oysters from the coast. In Cirencester, you could buy a ready-made mosaic floor.

British industries developed. There was a gold-mine in Wales, and there were a number of lead-silver mines. Romans in Italy imported British goods like corn, woollen cloaks and jewels. A drainpipe found at Pompeii was made of lead from the Mendip Hills.

▼ *Samian pottery like this bowl was an imported luxury item.*

This trade created wealth for the British to spend on luxuries from abroad. Imported goods on sale in the forum included coloured glassware, the shiny red pottery called *Samian*, lamps, wine and olives.

Tile-making was developed under the Romans. We can still read the graffiti scrawled by workers on tiles. At Dover one worker wrote: 'I made 551 tiles'. Someone added: 'I smashed 51'!

Some Roman foods were new to the Britons: peas, carrots, cucumbers, cabbages, walnuts, cherries, mulberries; and the figs which have been grown in warm parts of southern England ever since. One delicacy was stuffed dormouse. The Romans also made meat pies and the first British sausages. A heady blend of smells floated along the streets – of fish cooking, leather being tanned, hot bread and charcoal fumes.

A collection of wooden writing tablets was found at Vindolanda, a fort just south of Hadrian's wall. One tablet lists the delivery of 48 hubs, 48 axles, over 300 spokes, and 25 planks for beds. Another lists barley, beer, venison, pork and oysters.

◀ *Chariot races like this took place in amphitheatres in Britain. Disappearing round the corner is the* jubilator – *the pace-setter.*

A day in town could also include entertainment at the amphitheatre. At the *circus*, audiences watched unarmed criminals fighting off wolves, and gladiators fighting to the death. There were chariot races and boxing matches. Occasionally, at the theatre there might be touring companies performing plays.

Wagons were only allowed in the streets after dark. One can imagine the noise and confusion at night – with no police or streetlights!

▼ *A bronze skillet, or cooking pot, made in Britain in the third century. Bronze-smiths more often made toilet items like tweezers.*

17

This famous Roman pool can be seen at Bath, in Avon. Its original timber roof is no longer there, but the Roman pool's lead lining is still intact.

▲ *The Romans didn't use soap. Instead, they rubbed on oil from a small flask, and scraped off dirt with a strigil, like this one from Bath.*

Baths and Villas

The public baths were the social centre of many towns. The baths were generally used for getting clean, not swimming. At Silchester, the bather undressed in the *apodyterium*, a changing-room with lockers. The first bath was the *frigidarium*, which was cold; next came the warm *tepidarium*; and then the hot *caldarium*. Afterwards came a kind of sauna or steam-room, and finally another taste of the frigidarium for the tough.

There was an exercise yard too, to stroll and relax in, perhaps over a game of dice. Bathing must have taken hours.

Silchester baths were for local people, but the healing waters of Bath attracted people from all over the Roman Empire. On altars and tombstones, visitors' names are carved: Priscus from Gaul, Peregrinus from Germany.

The baths used enormous amounts of water. It came from rivers and springs, carried by aqueducts and lead pipes. Lincoln's water came from a spring called Roaring Meg.

Another Roman fashion liked by wealthy Britons was the building of villas. A villa was a very large, luxurious house at the centre of an estate or farm. It was usually oblong in shape. Some very large examples were built in the form of courtyards with mosaic floors, wall-paintings, central heating and their own hot baths. Historians believe that some 20,000 wealthy people lived in luxury in villas.

At the other extreme were slaves, who were bought and sold at auction. Their owners had the right to put slaves to death and kill their unwanted children. Archaeologists digging at a villa at Hambleden, in Buckinghamshire, found the corpses of nearly one hundred newborn babies.

▼ *The Roman palace at Fishbourne has a number of beautiful mosaic floors with pictures of mythical and real creatures of the sea – dolphins, sea-horses, and 'sea-panthers' like this one.*

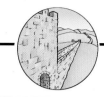
WHAT RELIGIOUS BELIEFS DID PEOPLE HAVE IN ROMAN BRITAIN?

Roman Britain was a place of many gods. The Romans worshipped the same gods as the Greeks, but gave them Roman names. The Greek god Hermes, for example, was renamed Mercury.

▲ *A stone image of the sun-god Mithras, found in a temple near Hadrian's Wall.*

Roman soldiers brought religions to Britain from all corners of the Empire. In London, archaeologists have dug up a temple to Mithras, a Persian god of light and truth. Mithras was popular with soldiers, and with rich merchants as a god of fair dealing. At least five other temples devoted to Mithras have been found in Britain.

The Romans were happy to worship two or three gods at one site. A worshipper might call and make offerings to all of them. Under the temple to Mithras in London was found a bust of Serapis, an Egyptian god of fertility. At Bruton in Somerset, archaeologists have found bronze statuettes of Hercules, Minerva and Mercury.

◀ *This lead 'curse-tablet' was offered to the gods at Bath by a heart-broken lover: 'May he who stole Sylvia from me waste away like the waters. May he become dumb.'*

The Romans had many gods, but the Britons had even more. Inscriptions to more than fifty Celtic gods have been found, many of them at springs and rivers. These local gods are sometimes mentioned in Roman inscriptions. The Romans tolerated the religions of people they conquered. This was partly because they thought of other people's gods as Roman gods in disguise!

▲ *This figure found in the River Thames is the Egyptian god Horus, who the Romans called Harpocrates. The finger at his mouth stands for silence, and he was sometimes placed at a temple entrance: 'Quiet please!'*

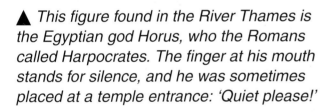

Sometimes the Romans adapted Celtic temples. At Hayling Island, in Sussex, the Britons had worshipped in a round timber hut. The Romans added a tiled floor and porch, and surrounded it with stone walls. It was now a 'Romano-British' temple.

Like people everywhere, the inhabitants of Roman Britain made offerings to their gods. At some temples they seem to have dropped copper coins along the path to the temple. At the altar they left small statues, pots or jewels. Sheep or goats were offered in sacrifice, and at Uley in Gloucestershire 150,000 animal bones have been found.

▲ *'Lares and penates' were Roman gods of the household. Lares, like this tiny, bronze statuette, guarded the home and the family's fields. Penates were spirits of the kitchen.*

Healing

We can easily work out the purpose of some Roman temples. At the ruins of one in Lydney overlooking the Severn were found models of dogs, animals the Romans associated with healing. Also found were an eye-doctor's stamp, and a model of an arm – to show the gods which part of the body was in need of healing.

▲ *This figure from Bath may be the head of a Gorgon – a Greek and Roman monster – but some writers believe it is the head of Sulis, a water god of the British Celts.*

At Bath, the Romans combined the worship of Minerva, the Roman goddess of healing, and the Celtic god Sulis. The spring was called Aquae Sulis Minerva: the spring of Sulis Minerva. Visitors came to Bath from all parts of Europe, to bathe in the healing waters of its hot springs. Over a million litres of water surge up from the ground there every day.

▶ *The warm water surging from rock beneath Bath was believed to cure arthritis, which was a common complaint in Roman Britain.*

Bath prospered. In the late first century AD, saunas, Turkish sweat rooms and a huge, hot swimming bath were built. The 'pool' had been invented, for customers to stroll round and lie about gossiping when they weren't in the water. But coins and jewellery thrown into the baths show that the tourists were still thinking of the gods and their healing powers.

Christianity

One of the many religions brought to Britain by the Romans was Christianity, which was introduced in the third century. Its early followers were persecuted, but the belief spread rapidly under Roman rule.

◀ Funeral urns like this one unearthed in Britain show that some Romans cremated their dead.

One Roman religion was emperor-worship. When the emperor Claudius died in AD 54, he was made a god. A huge temple was built to Claudius the god at Colchester.

At a villa in Hinton St Mary, Dorset, is a mosaic of the face of Christ, and behind it the Chi-Rho symbol – the first two letters of Christ's name in the Greek alphabet. Other objects found in the earth show this Chi-Rho symbol. Some are expensive silver objects, but others, like tiles, pots and cups, seem to have been offered by poorer people.

When the pagan Anglo-Saxons invaded Roman Britain, many Christians fled to the hills. There, they kept the Christian faith alive, to become perhaps the most important Roman contribution to British heritage.

▼ A fourth-century wall-painting from one of the earliest Christian chapels at Lullingstone Villa in Kent.

chapter seven

WHAT ART AND LITERATURE
DID THE ROMANS LEAVE US?

Soon after the Roman invasion, the first schools opened in British cities. Tacitus writes that the Emperor Agricola 'sent the sons of the British chieftains to school so that, instead of hating the Latin language, the Britons were eager to speak it fluently'. At the sites of Roman schools have been found inkwells, parchment and wax tablets which were written on with a sharp pen called a *stylus*.

The British had to adopt the Romans' language, Latin, to participate fully in the Roman way of life. Many modern English words have a Latin origin. 'Street' comes from 'strata' which means paved. A Roman 'centurion' commanded 100 soldiers, and 100 years is called a 'century'. These words come from the Latin 'centum' which means 100. Latin is still taught in some schools, and is used for terms in science and medicine.

▲ *The most enduring Roman works of art were mosaics crafted from hundreds of tiny, coloured fragments of stone and glass. This one decorated a London street, and shows Bacchus, god of wine, riding a tiger.*

Latin was the language of Roman law, and is still used in legal phrases today. The idea of a fair legal system comes from the Romans, and the word 'justice' comes from the Latin word for law. Cicero spoke of laws which 'cannot be bent by influence or broken by power or spoiled by money'.

The Romans loved art, literature and poetry – which they recited in their homes, in the streets and at the baths. They were influenced by Greek writing, which was first translated into Latin by the Roman writer Cicero. He also left behind 800 letters which tell us about Roman life and contain phrases which we still use, such as, 'There is no place like home'. His writing also influenced later British history. Queen Elizabeth I read all of Cicero's works while she was still a teenager.

▲ *Marcus Tullius Cicero wrote many essays, speeches and letters before being murdered for speaking out against Julius Caesar's successor, Mark Anthony.*

Cicero believed history to be very important: 'Not to know what happened before we were born is to remain perpetually a child. For what is the worth of human life unless it is woven into the life of our ancestors by the records of history.'

There were many great Roman writers and poets. Virgil, who wrote a long poem about the Roman Empire called *The Aeneid*, and Ovid, whose *Metamorphoses* is a collection of fantastic myths, influenced British writers like Keats and Shakespeare.

Our calendar was introduced by Julius Caesar, and we still use Roman numerals (I, II, III). Even our alphabet was inherited from the Romans.

▲ *This Roman wall-painting shows a music lesson. Julius Caesar told Cicero: 'It is a nobler thing to enlarge the boundaries of human intelligence than those of the Roman Empire.'*

chapter eight

WHY DID THE ROMANS
LEAVE BRITAIN?

▲ *A craftsman built this mosaic of a sea god into a pavement at Verulamium, in St Albans, between AD 160 and 190 – long before Anglo-Saxon soldiers came to live in the town.*

Whenever there was trouble in the Roman Empire, soldiers might be pulled out of Britain to deal with it. This weakened Britain's defences, and raiders attacked: Saxons from Europe, Picts from Scotland, Scots from Ireland.

The attacks were mostly hit and run raids, but in AD 367 the enemies of Britain all attacked together. For a year there was chaos. Hadrian's Wall was overrun by Picts. In the fire-blackened ruins of one of its towers have been found skeletons of men, women and children.

Saxons and Franks overwhelmed coastal forts in the east and south. Many villas were burnt. There was little the British could do to defend themselves. As fighters they were completely out of practice. For 300 years, only Roman soldiers had been allowed to carry arms.

Around AD 367, new houses were built at St Albans. Anglo-Saxon soldiers had been hired in the emergency, and given land in return for fighting against Rome's enemies. Some of the houses must have been built for them.

Long-distance trade slowed down. Industries in pottery, glass and mosaics started to close. No Roman coins bearing dates after AD 402 have been dug up in Britain.

In AD 410, the Goths attacked and burnt Rome. The last Roman soldiers in Britain were called home. The emperor, Honorius, gave the natives of Britain permission to carry arms for the first time since the conquest 350 years before. In other words, he was saying, from now on look after yourselves.

Many Romans who had settled in Britain stayed on, but this was the end of Roman rule. In many towns, baths and theatres no longer existed. In some towns, grass grew in the streets.

▲ *This gold coin shows Emperor Honorius. Minted in Milan before AD 402, it was one of the last Roman coins to enter Britain.*

▼ *Roman ships were based. here at Portchester Castle, in Hampshire. A Roman map shows this as one of the forts defending Britain against attacks from the sea.*

chapter nine

WHAT SURVIVES
OF THE ROMANS?

The Romans are still here. Hadrian's Wall winds its way high across the north of England from coast to coast. Imagine winter with snow on the hills and a biting wind from the east, and it is not hard to see lines of half-frozen soldiers staggering under the weight of stone blocks.

Today, you can imagine the Roman world like that – far off. But it is still really a near-at-hand world. Pieces of the Roman world turn up when motorways are being built; other pieces are lost for ever, buried under concrete. We find domestic items which give us a taste of Roman life: shoes, ink-pots, mirrors, toys from a child's grave.

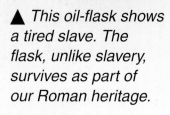

▲ This oil-flask shows a tired slave. The flask, unlike slavery, survives as part of our Roman heritage.

► Hadrian's Wall in the winter. The soldier stationed here would have appreciated the underpants sent to him from home!

You can still visit Roman villas and palaces to admire their mosaics, baths and underfloor heating. In York you can stand inside a Roman drain. On Hadrian's Wall you can try a Roman toilet for size. London, Canterbury and Chichester have remained occupied since Roman times.

Huge numbers of Roman military objects survive: bits of sword, helmets, armour. Relics of their industries include tiles, pots, lead pipes and a carpenter's plane.

The Romans left us a lighthouse at Dover, a sign of the sea-routes they founded. We still travel the long, straight roads that were essential to their Empire. Signposts and milestones were also Roman inventions.

The way we live comes from our Roman heritage. Perhaps our liking for towns and shopping precincts is Roman. Under the Romans, the British had their first taste of 'modern' town life. It was our first experience of living at peace in a unified land.

▲ *The Roman lighthouse at Dover.*

Around AD 304 in Verulamium, a Roman soldier, Alban, was beheaded for sheltering a Christian who had converted him. The town of St Albans grew up around the shrine of Alban, who was the first English martyr.

GLOSSARY

Amphitheatre A round open-air arena for sports, contests and plays.

Aqueducts Bridges which carry water.

Archaeologists People who study remains from ancient times.

Barbarians Uncivilized tribes.

Barracks A building used to house soldiers.

Basilica A Roman public hall containing law courts.

Britons People inhabiting Britain before the Roman conquest.

Celts An ancient European race of people including pre-Roman inhabitants of Britain and Gaul.

Centurion A commander of a troop of 100 Roman soldiers.

Chariot A two-wheeled vehicle pulled by horses, used in war and racing.

Circus Sports and games performed in an amphitheatre.

Decimation Killing of large numbers, originally one man in ten.

Druids Celtic priests.

Fortifications Buildings which strengthen defences against attack.

Forum A public square.

Gladiator A man trained to fight with weapons at Roman shows.

Goths A tribe from Germany.

Granary A storehouse for grain.

Imperial Belonging to an empire.

Imported Brought into the country from abroad.

Legion A large troop, originally 3000-6000, of Roman soldiers.

Milestone A stone beside a road showing the distance to a town.

Mosaic A picture created from tiny fragments of coloured glass or stone.

Pagan A believer in a faith other than the main religions of the world.

Palisade A fence of wooden stakes.

Scale Armour Armour made from scales of metal.

Strigil A skin-scraper used by bathers.

Toga A Roman citizen's loose, outer garment.

Tribute A payment made by people to a ruler or conqueror.

Triumph The parade into Rome of a victorious general.

Woad A plant which can be used to create blue dye.

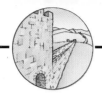

BOOKS TO READ

Chrisp, Peter *Family Life in Roman Britain* (Wayland, 1994)
Deary, Terry *Rotten Romans* (Scholastic, 1994)
Hall, Jenny and Jones, Christine *Roman Britain* (BBC, 1992)
James, Simon *Ancient Rome* (Dorling Kindersley Eyewitness Guides, 1991)
Hull, Robert *Roman Stories* (Wayland, 1993)

PLACES TO VISIT

Hadrian's Wall

The Museum of Antiquities in Newcastle University has a collection of inscriptions from the wall. You can visit well-preserved forts and museums at places such as Chesters, Housesteads and Vindolanda, all parts of the wall in Northumberland.

Verulamium Museum

St Albans, Hertfordshire.

The museum recreates life in Roman Britain using the remains of city walls, an amphitheatre and the foundations of shops.

Bath Roman Museum

Abbey Churchyard, Bath, Avon.

Site of the famous baths.

Fishbourne Roman Palace

Salthill Road, Chichester, West Sussex.

The remains of the first century palace contain fine mosaics and a replanted Roman garden.

Lullingstone Roman Villa

Lullingstone Park, Sevenoaks, Kent.

The remains of a Roman country villa contain one of the oldest Christian chapels in Britain.

There are Roman sites like the ones in the book throughout Britain. These include Hardknott Fort, Cumbria and Portchester Castle, Hampshire. There are almost certainly remains of Roman buildings or roads near your home that you could visit.

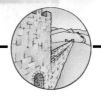

INDEX

Numbers in **bold** refer to pictures

Picture acknowledgements
The publishers would like to thank the following for permitting the reproduction of their pictures: British Museum 7(bottom), 16(bottom), 17(bottom), 21(right), 23(top), 25(bottom), 28(top); C.M.Dixon 4, 5, 7(top), 11(bottom), 12(top), 15, 16(top), 21(left), 27; Robert Harding *cover* (centre), *title page*, 10, 12-13(bottom), 14, 18(top), 22, 28-29(bottom); Michael Holford *cover* (surrounding images), 2-3, 6, 8(top), 17(top), 18(bottom), 19, 20, 23(bottom), 24, 26, 29(top); Wayland Picture Library 8-9, 11(top), 25(top). Maps on pages 9 and 13 are by Peter Bull Design.